Pebble® Plus

ICE AGE ANIMALS

Ancient Armadillos

by Jeni Wittrock

Consulting Editor: Gail Saunders-Smith, PhD

Content Consultant: Margaret M. Yacobucci, PhD
Education and Outreach Coordinator,
Paleontological Society; Associate Professor,
Department of Geology, Bowling Green State University

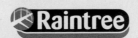

Raintree

Raintree is an imprint of Capstone Global Library Limited, a company incorporated in
England and Wales having its registered office at 7 Pilgrim Street, London, EC4V 6LB –
Registered company number: 6695582

www.raintree.co.uk
myorders@raintree.co.uk

Editorial Credits
Peggie Carley and Janet Kusmierski, designers; Wanda Winch, media researcher; Laura
Manthe, production specialist

ISBN 978 1 4062 9369 2
18 17 16 15 14
10 9 8 7 6 5 4 3 2 1

British Library Cataloguing in Publication Data
A full catalogue record for this book is available from the British Library.

Photo Credits
Illustrator: Jon Hughes
Shutterstock: Alex Staroseltsev, snowball, April Cat, icicles, Kotkoa, cover background, Leigh
Prather, ice crystals, pcruciatti, interior background

Every effort has been made to contact copyright holders of material reproduced in this book.
Any omissions will be rectified in subsequent printings if notice is given to the publisher.

All the Internet addresses (URLs) given in this book were valid at the time of going to press.
However, due to the dynamic nature of the Internet, some addresses may have changed, or
sites may have changed or ceased to exist since publication. While the author and publisher
regret any inconvenience this may cause readers, no responsibility for any such changes can
be accepted by either the author or the publisher.

Printed in China by Nordica.
0914/CA21401504

Contents

Tales of giants

It's a fight! Two big armadillos swing their heavy tails. Thud! Tail spikes smack the tough shells. But the spikes barely leave a mark.

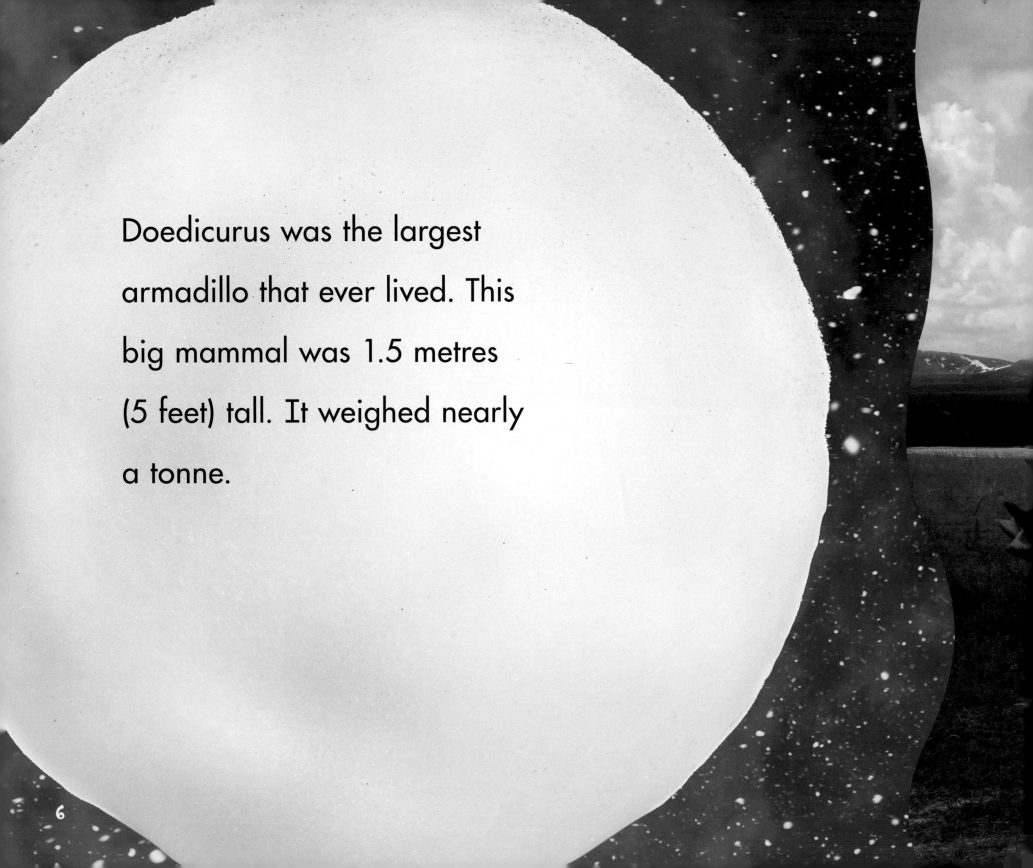

Doedicurus was the largest armadillo that ever lived. This big mammal was 1.5 metres (5 feet) tall. It weighed nearly a tonne.

These creatures roamed North
and South America long ago.
Ancient armadillos grazed
in grasslands and woodlands
during the Ice Age.

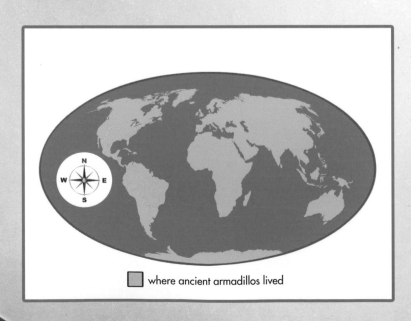

where ancient armadillos lived

Tough armour

Ancient armadillos had brown-grey bodies. Their shells were made up of bony scales called scutes. Tough scales covered armadillos' heads, too.

The armadillos had short legs and moved slowly. Their bumpy teeth were perfect for chewing grass and other plants. Spikes topped the ends of their tails.

The armadillos looked tough, but they did not hunt other animals. Their strong armour protected them from predators such as sabretooth cats.

Baby armadillos

Like armadillos today, ancient
armadillos were mammals.
A young Doedicurus stayed
with its mother. She fed and
protected her baby.

17

Changing times

Over time, Earth warmed up. Life became hard for the armadillos. The plants they ate died off. More predators hunted the armadillos.

Doedicurus became extinct
about 10,000 years ago.
Today's sloths and armadillos
are their relatives.

Glossary

armour protective covering

extinct no longer living; an extinct animal is one that has died out, with no more of its kind

graze eat grass and low plants

Ice Age time when much of Earth was covered in ice; the last ice age ended about 11,500 years ago

mammal warm–blooded animal

mate join together to make young

predator animal that hunts other animals for food

protect keep safe

relative part of the same family

scute one of many tough, plate-like scales that cover and protect an animal's body

smack hit

spike sharp, horn-like body part

Read more

First Encyclopedia of Dinosaurs and Prehistoric Life (Usborne First Encyclopedias), Sam Taplin (Usborne Publishing Ltd, 2011)

The Ice Age Tracker's Guide, Adrian Lister and Martin Ursell (Frances Lincoln Children's Books, 2010)

A Weekend With Dinosaurs (Fantasy Field Trips), Claire Throp (Raintree, 2014)

Websites

www.bbc.co.uk/nature/prehistoric
All you need to know about prehistoric life!

www.nhm.ac.uk/kids-only/dinosaurs
Find out everything you need to know about prehistoric life. Look at 3-D dinosaurs, learn fun facts, play games, and take a quiz!

Index